Edward Robeson Taylor, José-Maria de Heredia

Sonnets of José-Maria de Heredia. Done into English by Edward Robeson Taylor

Edward Robeson Taylor, José-Maria de Heredia

Sonnets of José-Maria de Heredia. Done into English by Edward Robeson Taylor

ISBN/EAN: 9783337732905

Printed in Europe, USA, Canada, Australia, Japan

Cover: Foto ©ninafisch / pixelio.de

More available books at **www.hansebooks.com**

SONNETS OF
José-Maria de Heredia

Done into English by

Edward Robeson Taylor

SAN FRANCISCO: WILLIAM DOXEY, *at the*
Sign of the LARK . . M DCCC XCVII

TO MY FRIENDS

LEVI COOPER LANE AND PAULINE COOK LANE

THESE TRANSLATIONS

ARE AFFECTIONATELY INSCRIBED

PREFACE

"Les Trophées" (The Trophies) is a volume of poetry so entitled made up of the one hundred and eighteen sonnets here translated and of other poems with the following titles: "Le Serrement de Mains," "La Revanche de Diego Laynez," "Le Triomphe du Cid," and "Les Conquérants de l'Or."

The sonnets, however, make up much the greater part in quantity as well as in quality of "Les Trophées," and are, indeed, in matter of art quite incomparable and unique—the "central characteristic of these splendid sonnets" being, as Mr. Edmund Gosse says, "their technical perfection. There is nothing loose or ungirt, nothing said vaguely because it would take time and labor to be precise." What the poet designs, to again quote Mr. Gosse, "is no more than a rapid descent of the ages, with here and there a momentary revelation of some highly suggestive and entertaining scene, or incident, or personage, rapidly given and as rapidly withdrawn, but seen for that moment with all the precision and effulgence possible, so that in the dimness of the grey past this one figure or incident may blaze out like a veritable luminary. For this purpose, everything needless, trifling or accidental, every triviality of expression, every superfluous phrase or image, must be rigidly suppressed. In so sudden and brief a revelation every touch must burn."

José-Maria de Heredia, as Mr. Gosse tells us, is a Cuban by birth and a Frenchman by education, his mother being French, while on his father's side "he is the direct descendant of that Adelantado don Pedro de Heredia, who came to America in the company of the second Admiral Diego Columbus, and who founded Cartagena in the West Indies." It is this ancestor to whom reference is made in the Conquerors series of the sonnets. He was born on the 22d of November, 1842, and is a member of the French Academy. Mr. Gosse devotes an interesting paper to the poet in his "Critical Kit-Kats" which is well worth one's reading. In his opinion, there delivered, Heredia is "beyond all question a great poetic artist and probably the most remarkable now alive in Europe."

In the construction of his sonnets the poet has adhered rigidly to that particular form without which no sonnet can be said to be good literary art. In every one of them you will find in the octet two quatrains, and in the sestet two tercets, and each will be found to be perfect in itself, with each contributing in due proportion to a determinate artistic unity. He never employs more than two rhymes in the octet, and in every instance, without exception, he rhymes the first, fourth, fifth and eighth lines with each other, and the second, third, sixth and seventh lines with each other. In the sestet he employs (except in a few instances where but two are used) three rhymes, these being distributed in a variety of ways; but in most of the sonnets the arrangement is: a-a-b-c-b-c or a-a-b-c-c-b. He follows the privilege of his Italian model in rhyming words which have the same articulate sound but different meanings, and in fact in one sonnet ("Le Tombeau du Conquérant") we have the rhyme of the octet thus: catalpas, pétale, fatale, pas, trépas, Occidentale, s'étale, pas; and in fact such rhymes occur frequently in his work. This privilege is exercised to a very limited extent by the English and American sonneteer, the genius of the language, perhaps, not lending itself gracefully or at least successfully to it—which, perhaps, may be subject of some lament, as the English language is not rich in rhyme.

In the versions here presented the form, including the rhyme arrangement, has been rigidly followed. In several of the versions two rhymes have been employed in the sestet instead of the three of the original, but the arrangement of the rhyme is, in these instances, the same as that of the original.

E. R. T.

San Francisco
September 1897.

TABLE OF CONTENTS

To José-Maria de Heredia 1

GREECE AND SICILY

Oblivion 5
HERCULES AND THE CENTAURS 7
    Nemea 9
    Stymphalus 10
    Nessus 11
    The Centauress 12
    Centaurs and Lapithæ 13
    Flight of the Centaurs 14
The Birth of Aphrodite 15
Jason and Medea 16
The Thermodon 17
ARTEMIS AND THE NYMPHS 19
    Artemis 21
    The Chase 22
    Nymphæa 23
    Pan 24
    The Bath of the Nymphs 25
The Vase 27
Ariadne 28
Bacchanal 29
The Awakening of a God 30
The Magician 31

The Sphinx	32
Marsyas	33
PERSEUS AND ANDROMEDA	35
Andromeda with the Monster	37
Perseus and Andromeda	38
The Ravishment of Andromeda	39
EPIGRAMS AND BUCOLICS	41
The Goatherd	43
The Shepherds	44
Votive Epigram	45
Funerary Epigram	46
The Shipwreck	47
The Prayer of Death	48
The Slave	49
The Husbandman	50
To Hermes Criophorus	51
The Youthful Dead	52
Regilla	53
The Runner	54
The Charioteer	55
On Othrys	56

ROME AND THE BARBARIANS

For Virgil's Ship	59
A Little Villa	60
The Flute	61
To Sextius	62
THE GOD OF THE GARDENS	63
I. *Come not! Away!*	65
II. *Respect, O Traveller,*	66
III. *Cursed Children, Ho!*	67
IV. *Enter. Fresh coated have my pillars been,*	68
V. *How Cold!*	69

Tepidarium	70
Tranquillus	71
Lupercus	72
The Trebia	73
After Cannæ	74
To a Triumpher	75
ANTONY AND CLEOPATRA	77
The Cydnus	79
Evening of Battle	80
Antony and Cleopatra	81
EPIGRAPHIC SONNETS	83
The Vow	85
The Spring	86
The Beech-Tree God	87
To the Divine Mountains	88
The Exiled	89

THE MIDDLE AGE AND THE RENAISSANCE

Church Window	93
Epiphany	94
The Wood-worker of Nazareth	95
Medal	96
The Rapier	97
After Petrarch	98
On the Book of Loves of Pierre de Ronsard	99
The Beautiful Viole	100
Epitaph	101
Gilded Vellum	102
The Dogaressa	103
On the Old-Bridge	104
The Old Goldsmith	105
The Sword	106
To Claudius Popelin	107

Enamel	108
Dreams of Enamel	109
THE CONQUERORS	111
The Conquerors	113
Youth	114
Tomb of the Conqueror	115
In the Time of Charles Fifth, Emperor	116
The Ancestor	117
To a Founder of a City	118
To the Same	119
To a Dead City	120

THE ORIENT AND THE TROPICS

VISION OF KHEM. *I. Midday. The air burns,*	123
II. The Moon on Nilus	124
III. And the crowd grows,	125
The Prisoner	127
The Samurai	128
The Daimio	129
Flowers of Fire	130
Century Flower	131
Coral Reef	132

NATURE AND DREAM

Antique Medal	135
Funeral	136
Vintage	137
Siesta	138
THE SEA OF BRITTANY	139
A Painter	141
Brittany	142
Flowery Sea	143
Sunset	144

XII

THE SEA OF BRITTANY—*Continued*

Star of the Sea	145
The Bath	146
Celestial Blazon	147
Armor	148
Rising Sea	149
Sea Breeze	150
The Shell	151
The Bed	152
Death of the Eagle	153
More Beyond	154
The Life of the Dead	155
To the Tragedian Rossi	156
Michelangelo	157
On a Broken Marble	158

NOTES:

The Magician	161
The Charioteer	163
For Virgil's Ship	164
To Sextius	165
Lupercus	166
The Beautiful Viole	168
Vision of Khem	171
The Samurai	171
Brittany	171
Flowery Sea	171
Armor	172
Rising Sea	172

XIII

All ancient glory sleeps, and men forget,
Unless there comes the poet with his art,
The flower of arts; and pouring from his tongue
A mingled stream of wisdom, verse and song,
Records great deeds in strains that never die.
>   *(From Pindar's sixth Isthmian Ode*
>   *as translated by Hugh Seymour Tremenheere).*

    For the thing that one hath well said goeth forth with a voice unto everlasting; over fruitful earth and beyond the sea hath the light of fair deeds shined, unquenchable forever.
>   *(From Pindar's third Isthmian Ode*
>   *as translated by Ernest Myers).*

TO JOSÉ-MARIA DE HEREDIA

'Twas eagle-winged, imperial Pindar who
Sent down the ages on the tide of song
The thought that only to the years belong
Those deeds that win immortal poet's due.

His athletes living rise before the view
And strive fore'er by magic of his tongue;
Still shepherd's pipe and lay sound sweet and strong
As when Theocritus attuned them true.

And so through thee the feats of heroes great,
The hues of life of other times than ours,
With such refulgence in thy sonnets glow,

That in the splendor of their new estate,
They there, with deathless Art's supernal powers,
Shall o'er the centuries enchantments throw.

    San Francisco, California,
    May 31, 1897.

GREECE AND SICILY

OBLIVION

On headland's height the temple's ruins lie,
Where Death has intermixed bronze Heroes slain
With marble Goddesses whose glory vain
The lonely grass enshrouds with many a sigh.

Only at times a herdsman, driving by
His kine for drink, piping antique refrain
That floods the heavens to the very main,
Shows his dark form against the boundless sky.

Sweet mother Earth, all vainly eloquent,
Each springtime to the Gods acanthus green
Gives for the capitals that once have been;

But man, to old-time dreams indifferent,
Hears without tremor, in the midnight deep,
The ocean moaning as the sirens weep.

HERCULES AND THE CENTAURS

NEMEA

Since lonely Tamer plunged in forest drear
To spy the ground for every frightful trace,
Resounding roars have told the fierce embrace.
Now sinks the sun, and silence soothes the ear.

As herdsman toward Tirynthus flees in fear,
Through thicket, brier and brake he turns his pace,
And sees with eyes bulged from their orbit's space
At edge of wood the tawny monster rear.

He screams; for he beholds Nemea's bane
That on the blood-red heavens displays its mane,
And madly gnashes its tremendous teeth;

For shadows deepening in the twilight air,
With Hercules the horrid skin beneath—
Man blent with beast—make hideous vision there.

STYMPHALUS

The birds in swarming thousands far and near,
As he descends the foul declivity,
Sudden as squall in wingèd flight all flee
Above the dismal, agitated mere.

Some, flying low, in network cross nor fear
To brush the face oft kissed by Omphale;
Whereat, triumphal shaft adjusting, he,
Archer superb, strides through the reed-grass there.

Thenceforth the frighted, arrow-riddled cloud
Pours hideous flood, immixed with screamings loud,
And streaked with fiery bolts of murderous levin.

At last, the Sun across the thick cloud sees,
Through openings pierced by bow of Hercules,
The blood-drenched Hero smiling up to Heaven.

NESSUS

When I was living as my brothers were,
The better things or deeper ills unknown,
My roving rule Thessalian hills did own,
Whose icy torrents laved my vermeil hair.

Thus grew I in the sun, free, joyous, fair;
And nought my sleep disturbed or daily run,
Save when my nostrils breathed, nor wished to shun,
The ardent scent of the Epirus mare.

But since Stymphalian Archer's spouse I've seen
Smiling triumphantly his arms between,
My hairs are bristled and desires torment;

For that some God—cursed be his name and plan!—
Has in my loins' too feverous blood all blent
The lust of stallion with the love of man.

THE CENTAURESS

Of old, through torrents, valleys, woods and rocks,
The famous troop of countless Centaurs strayed;
Upon their sides the sun with shadows played;
Their dark hair mingled with our flaxen locks.

Choked are the caves, and summer's grass but mocks,
For lonely now we press its springing blade;
And times there are when in the night's warm shade
The stallion's distant cry my bosom shocks.

For, day by day diminished on the earth
The mighty sons to whom the Cloud gave birth,
Woman distraught forsakes us and pursues.

Their love thus prompts us to the brute's base fare:
The cry which draws us is a neigh that woos,
And their desire for us is that of mare.

CENTAURS AND LAPITHAE

Now rushes to the feast the nuptial tide—
Centaurs and warriors, drunken, daring, fair;
And flesh heroic, in the torch's glare,
Mix with the Cloud's own children side by side.

Jests, tumult... A cry!...'Gainst spoiler's breast the Bride
Struggles 'neath purple rent to fragments there,
To shock of hoofs the brass rings through the air,
And thunderous shouts o'er wreck and ruin ride.

Then one with whom the greatest are but clowns
Upsprings. His head a lion's muffle crowns,
Bristling with hairs of gold. 'Tis Hercules.

Whereat, from end to end of that vast space,
Cowed by the fury of that wrathful face,
The monstrous, guilty troop reluctant flees.

FLIGHT OF THE CENTAURS

Straight for the Mount where they may safely rest,
Glutted with slaughter and revolt, they fly;
Fears lash them on, they feel 'tis now to die,
And lion's odor does the night infest.

The hydra, stellion trampling on, they breast
Ravines, woods, torrents, as they hurry by,
And now appears against the distant sky
Olympus', Ossa's, or black Pelion's crest.

At times, some bold one of the band is seen
To sudden prance, turn back, look round, and then
Rejoin his brethren with a single bound;

For there the full, all dazzling moon has made
Extend behind them—nought could more confound—
The giant horror of Herculean shade.

THE BIRTH OF APHRODITE

Chaos at first ruled all the worlds, and there
They formless rolled, unknowing Time or Space;
Then Gæa gave her sons, the Titan race,
Her mighty bosom rich beyond compare.

They fell. The Styx enveloped them; and e'er,
Beneath the wondering ether, Spring's sweet face
Unfolds its beauty to the sun's embrace,
And golden harvests feel the Summer's care.

Savage, by laughter and by sports unblessed,
The Immortals held Olympus' snowy crest.
But the heavens caused to fall the virile dew;

And Ocean parts; then Aphrodite nude
Emerges radiant from the foaming blue,
And blossoms there in Uranus' rich blood.

JASON AND MEDEA

To Gustave Moreau.

Beneath domed foliage, in enchanted spell
Of soundless calm—cradle of fears of yore—
Round them rare dawn its brightening tears shed o'er
Bloom rich and strange beyond all parallel.

In magic air where poisonous perfumes dwell
She sowed such charms from out her potent store,
The Hero, weaponed by her matchless lore,
Shook off the lightnings from the illustrious Fell.

Illumining the wood with gemlike showers,
Great birds immingled under vaults of flowers,
And silvery lakes drank deep of azure skies.

Love smiled upon them; but the fatal Fair
Bore with her and her jealous wrath's despair
Philters of Asia, father, Deities.

THE THERMODON

Where Themiscyra blazes, that has e'er
Trembled since morn with clash of horsemen dread,
Dark, sad and slow, Thermodon bears the dead,
The arms, the chariots, death would not spare.

Phillippis, Phœbe, Marpe, Aella, where,
Who, by Asteria and Hippolyt' led,
With royal squadron found a slaughterous bed?
Their pale, disheveled bodies now lie there.

Such giant lily bloom is here laid low,
Both shores the warriors high-heaped bestrow,
Where neighs, at times, and vainly strives, a horse;

And the Euxine sees at dawn far up the flood
Ensanguined, from its mouth unto its source,
White stallions flying red with virgins' blood.

ARTEMIS AND THE NYMPHS

ARTEMIS

With wood's spiced scents perfuming every space,
Thine ample nostrils dilate, Huntress bright,
And in thy virginal and virile might,
Thy locks thrown back, thou startest on the chase.

And with the roaring of the leopard race
Thou mak'st Ortygia's isle resound till night,
And o'er the orgy of the hounds leap'st light
That lie ripped open on the sparse, red grass.

But most thou joyest, when the bramble bites
And tooth or claw thy glorious body smites,
To see the avenging iron draw sanguine rain;

For thy heart would the cruel sweetness dare
Of mixing an immortal purple there
With black and hideous blood of monsters slain.

THE CHASE

The chariot to the horses' flying feet
Heaven's highest mounts, their hot breath making glow
The golden plains that undulate below;
And Earth lies basking in the flaming heat.

In vain the forest's leaves in masses meet:
The Sun, where hills their hazy summits show,
In shade where silvery fountains laughing flow,
Steals, darts and glints, in victory complete.

'Tis the hour flamboyant when, through brake and brier,
Bounding superb with her Molossians dire,
Midst cries of death, hoarse clamorings and blood,

Her shafts swift sending from the tightened string,
With locks wide streaming, breathless, conquering,
Impassioned, Artemis affrights the wood.

NYMPHÆA

In westward flight the car of heavenly mould
Speeding toward the horizon's verge, in vain
The powerless God pulls back with fourfold rein
His horses plunging in the glowing gold.

It sinks. The sea's hoarse moanings manifold
Fill the deep heaven where creeps the purple's sheen,
While silently in evening's blue serene
The Crescent in her silver now is stoled.

It is the hour that Nymphs, where springs gush clear,
Throw the slack bow the empty quiver near.
Save distant belling of a stag, all's still.

The dance whirls on beneath the tepid moon,
And Pan, with slow and then with faster tune,
Laughs as the reeds, beneath his breathing, thrill.

PAN

Across the brake, by ways that hidden lie
At foot of where the verdant pathways run,
Divine Nymph hunter, the Goat-footed one,
Steals through the forest with an ardent eye.

'Tis sweet to hear the freshening sound, the sigh,
Rising from viewless springs at summer's noon,
When the bright vanquisher of clouds, the Sun,
His golden arrows at the dark lets fly.

A Nymph lone wandering stays her step. She hears
Fall drop by drop the morning's lovely tears
Upon the moss. Her heart drinks ecstasies.

But, with a single bound, outsprings the God,
Enclasps her, then with mocking laughter flees...
And silence settles over all the wood.

THE BATH OF THE NYMPHS

From the Euxine sheltered is a vale where grows
Above the spring a leaning laurel tree,
From which a pendant Nymph in frolic glee
Touches the gelid pool with timorous toes.

Her sisters, challenged by the shells where flows
The gushing wave they sport with joyously,
Plunge deep, and from the foam a hip gleams free,
And from bright locks, a bust or bosom's rose.

The great, dark wood is filled with mirth divine.
Sudden, two eyes within the shadow shine.
The Satyr 'tis!... His laugh benumbs their play;

And forth they dart. So, at a crow's ill cry,
Caÿster's snowy swans in wild array
Above the river all distracted fly.

THE VASE

A cunning hand has carved this ivory so:
Here all the wealth of Colchis' forests lies,
With Jason, and Medea of magic eyes,
And on a stela's top the Fleece's glow.

Near them we see the immortal Nilus flow,
And more remote, Bacchants, in merry wise,
With clustering vine's entwining greeneries
Enwreathe the resting bulls' unyoking bow.

Beneath, are cavaliers that hack and slay,
The dead upon their bucklers borne away,
The old that wail, and mothers' tearful face.

For handles apt, Chimæras, who, with breast
All firm and white against the edges pressed,
Forever drink from the exhaustless vase.

ARIADNE

To vibrant clash of cymbal's brass the Queen,
In lovely nudeness on great tiger's back,
Views, with the revels which illume his track,
Iacchus coming o'er the strand amain.

The royal monster treads the sandy plain,
To weight adored submitting, when, alack,
Touched by her hand from which the rein falls slack,
He bites his bridle's flowers in passion's pain.

Letting the clusters of her amber hair
Roll to his side where grapes hang luscious there,
His roaring dies away and moves her not.

In sooth, her mouth, steeped in ambrosial bliss,
Its cries to faithless lover now forgot,
Yearns for the Asian Tamer's nearing kiss.

BACCHANAL

A clamor loud the Ganges fills with fright:
The tigers from their yokes have torn away,
And, fiercely mewing, bound; while in dismay
Bacchants crush down the vintage in their flight.

The fruited vines, mangled by claw and bite,
Spatter the striped ones with their reddening spray
Near where the leopards, leaping to the fray,
Roll in the purple mire their bellies white.

Upon their writhing bodies the dazed deer,
Their hoarse cries sinking into rattle low,
Smell the blood crimsoning the sunlight's glow.

But the mad God, with shout and thyrsus there,
Cheers the strange sport, and mixes—added bale—
The howling female with the roaring male.

THE AWAKENING OF A GOD

With bruisèd throat, their tresses flowing free,
Their grieving goaded by the tears that rise,
The Byblus women with lugubrious cries
Conduct the slow and mournful obsequy.

For on the couch, heaped with anemone,
Where death has closed his languishing, large eyes,
Perfumed with spices and with incense, lies
The one whom Syria's maids loved doatingly.

The singers sound the dirge till morning breaks.
But look! now at Astarte's call he wakes—
She who bedews the cinnamon's sweet wood.

He's risen, the antique youth! and all the heaven
Blossoms in one great rose tinted with blood
Of an Adonis to celestials given.

THE MAGICIAN

Eachwhere, even at the altars I embrace,
She calls, her pleading arms my vision fill.
O sire revered, O mother who did will
To bear me, am not I of hateful race?

The vengeful Eumolpidus in Samothrace
Shakes not his red robes at my threshold, still,
I fly faint-hearted, leaden-footed, till
I hear the sacred dogs howl on my trace.

Where'er I feel or breathe, to me are nigh
The same black, odious spells, charms sinister,
The wrath of Gods once more has bound me by;

For they have irresistibly armed her
Intoxicating mouth and deep dark eye,
With which to slay me with her kiss and tear.

THE SPHINX

Buried beneath Cithæron's briers a way
Leads through the rock to centre, where,
With eyes of gold, and throat and belly rare,
Shines virgin eagle-winged whom none can sway.

The Man stops at the threshold, dazed.—What, pray,
Is this dark shadow glooming all my air?
—Love.—Art the God?—The Hero, I—Then dare;
But thou seek'st death. Durst thou have courage?—Yea;

Bellerophon subdued Chimæra dire.
—Come not.—Thou know'st my mouth sets thine on fire.
—Come then! Between mine arms thy bones I'll maim,

My talons tear thy flesh...—What's agony,
If I have raped thy kiss and conquered fame?
—Thy conquest's vain; thou diest.—O ecstasy!...

MARSYAS

Thy natal pines that raptured heard thy strains
Have burned thy flesh, O most unhappy one!
Thy bones are melted, and thy blood flows on
The wave the Phrygian Mount pours toward the plains.

The heavenly Citharist, who jealous reigns,
Has, with his plectrum, killed thy reeds, whose tone
O'er bird and beast its magic spell had thrown;
And of Celænæ's singer nought remains—

Nought but a bloody shred on yonder yew
Where the poor wretch his nameless horror knew.
O cruel God! O cries of that sweet voice!

Beneath a hand too wise no more you'll find
Mæander's stream the sighing flute rejoice,
For Marsyas' skin is plaything of the wind.

PERSEUS AND ANDROMEDA

ANDROMEDA WITH THE MONSTER

Cepheus' chaste one, her locks in disarray,
Chained to the isle's bleak crag of sunless gloom,
Bemoans in useless sobs her living tomb,
Her regal form to shuddering fears a prey.

The monstrous ocean with tempestuous sway
Spatters her icy feet with biting foam,
And her fast closing eyes, where'er they roam,
See countless, gleaming jaws their rage display.

Like thunder peal from out a cloudless sky
A sudden neighing rolls and echoes nigh.
Her eyes unclose. Horror and joy are one;

For she beholds, in whirling flight and free,
The wingèd horse, upbearing Zeus's son,
Cast his vast shade of azure on the sea.

PERSEUS AND ANDROMEDA

Midst seething foam bringing his flight to rein,
Medusa's and the monster's conqueror Knight,
Streaming with bloody spume of horrid sight,
The virgin golden-haired bears off amain.

On Chrysaor's brother, steed of sacred strain,
Who paws, and neighs, and rears in wild despite,
He seats the loved one, bashed, of desperate plight,
Who laughing clasps him tight, then sobs again.

He holds her close. Round them the surges play.
Feebly she draws her beauteous feet away
From where they flying kiss the billowy deep;

While Pegasus, inflamed by ocean's stings,
Obeys the Hero, and with bounding leap
Beats the dazed heavens with his flaming wings.

THE RAVISHMENT OF ANDROMEDA

The splendid wingèd horse, in silent flight,
From out his nostrils blowing clouds of fume,
Bears them with quivering of his every plume,
Across the starry ether and blue night.

Now Afric plunges from their soaring height,
Then Asia...desert...Libanus in tomb
Of mist and fog..and here, all white with spume,
The cruel sea that closed sweet Helle's sight.

Like two enormous cloaks the wind swells wide
The pinions which, as through the stars they glide,
Keep the clasped lovers nested from the cold;

While as their throbbing shadows they espy,
From Aries to Aquarius they behold
Their Constellations dawning in the sky.

EPIGRAMS AND BUCOLICS

THE GOATHERD

Follow not, shepherd, in that rough ravine,
That stupid goat's mad leaps; for on the side
Of Mænalus, where summer bids us bide,
Night rises quickly, so thy hope resign.

Rest here, wilt thou? I have both figs and wine.
All day this wild retreat have we espied.
Speak low, Mnasylus, Gods roam far and wide,
And Hecate views us with her eyes divine.

A Satyr's cave is yon dark gap below—
Familiar demon whom these summits know;
Perhaps he'll venture out, if quiet we.

Hear'st thou the pipe which sings upon his lip?—
'Tis he! His horns now catch the rays; and see,
He makes my goats in moonlight blithely trip.

THE SHEPHERDS

Come. Cyllene's gorges the path sinks in.
Behold his cave and spring; there is he fain
To sleep on thymy bed and wake his strain
Within the shadow of yon glorious pine.

The pregnant ewe to this old trunk confine.
Dost know, before a month, with lambkin then,
In cheese and milk she'll give him plenteous gain?
A mantle of her wool the Nymphs will spin.

Mayst be propitious, Pan!—Goat-footed one,
Who guard'st the flocks that on Arcadia run,
Thee I invoke...He hears! The tree gives sign.

The sun sinks down the radiant west. Depart.
The poor's gift, friend, is same as marble shrine,
If offered to the Gods with pure and simple heart.

VOTIVE EPIGRAM

To Ares harsh! To Eris strife-possessed!—
Help me, I'm old, to hang on pillar these:
My shield, my sword well hacked with braveries,
My broken helmet with its bloody crest.

Join there this bow.—But, say, is't meet I rest
The hemp around the wood,—hard medlar tree's
No arm but mine has ever bent with ease,—
Or stretch the cord again with eager zest?

The quiver also take. Thine eye cons o'er
The sheath of leather for the archer's store—
The arrows which the wind of battle floats.

'Tis empty; and thou think'st my shafts are gone?
Betake thee then to field of Marathon,
And there thou'lt find them in the Persians' throats.

FUNERARY EPIGRAM

Stranger, here lies the blithesome grasshopper
Young Helle guarded long from direful fate,
And whose wing, vibrant under foot serrate,
In bilberry, pine and cytisus did whir.

Alas! she's dead—the natural dulcimer,
Of furrow, field and corn the muse elate;
Lest thou disturb her slumber's peaceful state,
Pass quickly by, nor heavily press on her.

'Tis yonder. Midst a tuft of thyme we see
Her grave's white stone its beauty freshly rear.
What man escapes this highest destiny!

Her tomb is watered with a child's fond tear,
And every morn Aurora piously
With copious dewdrops makes libation there.

THE SHIPWRECK

With breeze astern and sky all cloudless he,
Just as Arcturus shows his rising sphere,
Sees the receding Pharos disappear,
Proud of his brass-lined ship's rapidity.

But Alexandria's mole no more he'll see:
In waste of sand no kid could pasture near
The tempest's hand has scooped his sepulchre,
Where now the wind makes whirling revelry.

In fold the deepest of the shifting dune,
In dawnless night where shines nor star nor moon,
At last the navigator quiet owns.

O Earth, O Sea, pity his anxious Shade!
And on the Hellenic shore where rest his bones
Thy tread be light, thy voice be silent made.

THE PRAYER OF DEATH

Stop!—Traveller, list to me. If thy step run
To Cypselus and to the Hebrus' shore,
Old Hyllus find and pray him to deplore
Fore'er and e'er his ne'er returning son.

My murdered flesh the wolves have feasted on;
The rest in this dark thicket lies; and o'er
The Erebus-gloomed banks great shadows pour
Indignant tears. My death's avenged by none.

Depart then; and if e'er at close of day
Thou seest, at grave's or hillock's foot, delay
A black-veiled woman reft of every bloom,

Approach; nor night nor charms need give thee fears;
It is my mother, who, on shadowy tomb,
Clasps a void urn and fills it with her tears.

THE SLAVE

All wretched, shocking, nude, with vilest fare,
Such slave am I—my body bears the signs—
Born free at foot of gulf whose beauteous lines
See honeyed Hybla his blue summits rear.

Alas! I left the happy isle....Ah! shouldst thou e'er
Toward Syracuse and bees and clustering vines
Follow the swans as winter's cold declines,
Good host, acquaint thee with my lovèd dear.

Shall I see more her dark, pure, violet eye
Reflecting smilingly her natal sky
Beneath that eyebrow's bow where hearts are slain?

Have pity!—Find my Clearista, pray;
Tell her I live to meet her once again;
Thou'lt surely know her, for she's sad alway.

THE HUSBANDMAN

The plough, seed-basket, yoke, and shining shares,
The pitchfork which so well the sheaves bestows,
The harrow, goad, the sharp-edged scythe that mows
In one short day a barn-floor-full of ears;

These tools familiar, now so hard he bears,
Old Parmis to the immortal Rhea vows,
Who the earthed seed with vital power endows.
For him, her task is o'er—he's four-score years.

For century nearly, in the burning sun,
He has pushed the coulter, yet no richer grown.
Joyless his life, remorse now knows him not;

But he is worn with labor, and he dreams
That, with the dead, toil still may be his lot
Where Erebus laves the fields with darksome streams.

TO HERMES CRIOPHORUS

That the companion of the Naiads may
Be pleased to bring the ewe the ram anigh,
So that through him might endless multiply
The browsing flocks that near Galæsus stray;

He should be gladdened with the feast's array
Beneath the herdsman's reedy canopy;
Sweet, sacrifice to the Divinity
On marble table or on block of clay.

Then honor Hermes; the sagacious God
Prefers pure hand that takes chaste victim's blood
To fane or altar with resplendence fraught.

Friend, raise on border of thy mead a mound,
And let the blood from hairy throat of goat
Purple the turf and darken there the ground.

THE YOUTHFUL DEAD

O living one, midst grasses quickly move
Of mound where lie my ashes in despair,
Nor the flowers trample of my grave from where
I list to ant and ivy creep above.

Thou stop'st? Thou heardst the coo of mourning dove.
Oh, on my tomb her sacrifice forbear;
Take not her beauty from the ambient air;
Life is so sweet, still let her taste thereof.

Thou knowest? Beneath the portal's myrtle wreath,
Virgin and spouse at nuptial shrine came death—
From all I loved so far, although so near.

My eyes respond not to the happy light,
And now inhabit I, alas! fore'er,
Remorseless Erebus and gloomy Night.

REGILLA

Annia Regilla, Aphrodite's own
And Ganymede's, in death sleeps here;
Æneas' daughter to Herodes dear.
So beauteous, happy, young, for her make moan.

The Shade, whose lovely body here lies lone,
With Prince of Islands of the Blest counts e'er
The days, the months, and long, long year,
Since banished far from all that she had known.

Her memory haunts her spouse, and unconsoled,
On purple bed of ivory and gold
He sleepless tosses and lamenting cries.

He comes not; and the spirit of the one
So loved, anxious, yet hoping for him, flies
Still round the sceptred Rhadamanthus' throne.

THE RUNNER

On a Statue by Myron.

As when at Delphi, Thymus close behind,
He flew through stadium to applause's roar,
So on this plinth now Ladas runs once more,
On bronze foot, slim, and swifter than the wind.

With arm outstretched, eyes fixed, trunk front inclined,
The beaded drops of sweat his face glide o'er;
Surely while sculptor did the metal pour,
The athlete leaped from mould in form designed.

He throbs, he trembles, hopes, yet fears to lose;
His side pants, the cleaved air his lips refuse,
And with the strain his muscles jutting rise.

His spirit's ardor is beyond control,
And passing o'er supporting base he flies
In the arena toward the palm and goal.

THE CHARIOTEER

Stranger, that one who stands on golden pole,
His steeds of black, in one hand four-fold rein,
In other whip of finest ashen grain,
Better than Castor can his car control.

Famous his sire, himself on honor's roll...
But see, he starts, the limit red to gain,
And strews his rivals o'er the arena's plain—
This Libyan bold dear to the Emperor's soul.

In the dazed circus toward the goal and palm,
Seven times around, the victor, cool and calm,
Has whirled.—All Hail, son of Calchas the Blue!

And thou mayst see (if that a mortal eye
The heaven-crowned car with wings of fire may view)
Once more to Porphyry glorious Victory fly.

ON OTHRYS

To Puvis de Chavannes.

The air blows fresh. The sun sinks gorgeously.
The kine fear not ox-fly's nor beetle's pest.
On Othrys' slopes the shadows lengthen.—Rest.
Dear guest sent by the Gods, rest here with me.

Whilst drinking foaming milk, thine eye shall see,
From threshold of my rural cot, the crest
Olympian, Tymphrestus' snowy breast,
The glorious mountains, fertile Thessaly,

Eubœa and the Sea; through twilight's crimson haze
Callidromus and Œta's top, where Hercules
Raised his first altar and his dreadful pyre;

And there below, Parnassus' glowing height,
Where Pegasus now folds his wings of fire,
To mount at dawning in immortal flight.

ROME AND THE BARBARIANS

FOR VIRGIL'S SHIP

May your kind stars guard well all dangers through,
Bright Dioscuri, Helen's kin divine,
The Latin poet who would fain see shine
The golden Cyclades amidst the blue.

May he have softest airs man ever knew;
May perfume-breathed Iapyx now incline
With swelling sails to speed him o'er the brine,
Until the foreign shore shall glad his view.

Through Archipelago where dolphins glide,
The Mantuan singer fortunately guide;
Lend him, O Cygnus' sons, fraternal ray.

One-half my love the fragile boat contains,
Which o'er the sea that heard Arion's lay
Bears glorious Virgil to the Gods' domains.

A LITTLE VILLA

Yes, that's the heritage of Gallus hoar
Thou dost on yon cisalpine hill divine;
His little house is sheltered by a pine;
Its single story thatch scarce covers o'er.

And yet for guest there lacks nor room nor store:
He has capacious oven for bread, the vine,
And in his garden ranks of lupin fine.
'Tis little? Gallus ne'er has longed for more.

His wood yields fagots through the winter hours,
And shade in summer under leafy bowers;
In autumn one some thrush may make his prize.

'Tis there, contented with his narrow round,
He ends his days upon his natal ground.
Go, now thou knowest why Gallus is so wise.

THE FLUTE

Evening is here. Some pigeons cross the sky.
Nothing so well an amorous fever chains
As when with pipe to lip its soothing strains
Blend with the rush-grown stream's fresh melody.

In shade of plane-tree where at ease we lie
The grass is soft. Let, friend, that goat which feigns
Indifference to the trembling kid she weans,
Climb up the rock and browse the herbage nigh.

With seven unequal stems of hemlock made,
Well joined with wax, my flute, or sharply played
Or grave, will weep, or moan, or joyous sing.

Come. Try Silenus' art that knows no death,
And thy sad sighs of love will take to wing
Amidst thy sacred pipe's harmonious breath.

TO SEXTIUS

Clear sky. The barque the sands has glided o'er;
The orchards bloom, and frost in silvery sheet
No longer glints from mead the morn to greet;
And ox and neatherd leave their stabled store.

All things revive.—But Death and his sad lore
Still press us; and the day thou'lt surely meet
When lucky cast of dice the royal seat
At revel's feast will ne'er allot thee more.

Life's short, O Sextius. Make haste to live;
Our weakened knees with age already strive.
In the cold land of Shades no springtime bides.

Come then. The woods are green, and season right
To immolate to Faunus, where he hides
In some dark haunt, black goat or lambkin white.

THE GOD OF THE GARDENS

To Paul Arène.

I

Olim truncus eram ficulnus.
HORACE.

Come not! Away! Let not one step be stayed!
Insidious pillager, I fancy you
Would steal the grapes, mad-apples, olives, too,
Which the sun ripens in the orchard's shade.

I watch.— A shepherd once with hedge-bill blade
Carved me from fig-tree trunk Ægina knew;
Laugh, but consider how Priapus grew,
And know none can his fierce revenge evade.

Of old, to seamen dear, on galley's beak
I stood erect, vermeil, and joyed to speak
To laughter-sparkling or foam-crested waves;

But now, of fruits and salads warder poor,
This garden I defend 'gainst roaming thieves...
The smiling Cyclades I'll ne'er see more.

II

Hujus nam domini colunt me Deumque salutant.
CATULLUS.

Respect, O Traveller, if my wrath you fear,
That humble roof of rush and flag above
A grandsire's and his children's mutual love;
He owns the close and spring that bubbles clear.

'Twas he who placed, amid the area here,
My emblem set in lime-tree's heart, to prove
His only God am I—sole guardian of
His orchard decked with flowers I hold most dear.

Rustic and poor, and yet devoted they;
For on my gaine they piously display
Poppy, green barley ears and violet;

And twice a year, by knife of planter slain,
The rural altar with the blood is wet
Of youthful, bearded goat of potent strain.

III

Ecce villicus
Venit...
                CATULLUS.

Cursed children, Ho! Of dog, of traps, beware!
As guardian here, I would not, for my sake,
Have one pretending garlic bulb to take
Plunder my fruit-groves, nor my bunches spare.

Below, the planter mows his field, from where
He spies you; if he comes here, by my stake!
With hard wood handled by his arm he'll make
Your loins well smoke, whatever God may care.

Quick, take the left-hand path, and keep it quite
To end of hedge where beech-tree woos the light;
Then take the word one slips into your ear:

A negligent Priapus lives near by;
His arbor pillars you can see from here,
Where the grapes blush midst shade of greenery.

IV

Mihi Corolla pieta vere ponitur.

CATULLUS.

Enter. Fresh coated have my pillars been,
And 'neath my arbor new, from sunshine's glare,
The shade is softest. Balm perfumes the air,
And April strews her flowers o'er all the scene.

By turns the seasons deck me: olives green,
Ripe grapes, bright chalices, the golden ear;
And vats the curd of morning milk still bear,
Which goats from out their udders kindly drain.

The master honors me. My worth I own:
Nor thrush nor thief marauds his vine; and none
Is better guarded in the Roman Land.

Sons fair, wife virtuous, the man at home,
Each eve from market, jingles in his hand
The deniers bright that he has brought from Rome.

V

Rigetque dura barba juncta crystallo.

Diversorum poetarum lusus.

How cold! On vine the frost is glittering;
I watch for sun, knowing the time exact
When dawn red tints Soracte's snows. All racked
Is rural God—man's so perverse a thing.

For twenty winters, lonely, shivering,
In this old close I've been. My beard's compact,
My paint scales off, my shrunken wood is cracked,
And now I dread of heartless verse the sting.

Why of Penates am I not, or Lar
Domestic even, retouched, unknown to care,
With fruits and honey gorged or decked alway?

In vestibule, the wax ancestors near,
I shall grow old; and on their virile day
The children's bullæ I shall have to wear.

TEPIDARIUM

O'er their soft limbs has myrrh its fragrance shed;
And bathed in warmth beneath December's skies
They dream, while the bronze lamp with flaming eyes
Throws light and shadow on each beauteous head.

On byssus cushions of empurpled bed
Some amber, rosy figure nerveless tries
To stretch, or bend, or from the couch to rise,
Where linen's folds voluptuously spread.

In nakedness, exhaling ardent fume,
An Asian woman mid the heated room
Twines her smooth arms in pliant, languorous play;

Ausonius' daughters, mad with ecstasy,
Drink in the rich and savage harmony,
As over blushless bust their dark locks stray.

TRANQUILLUS

C. Plinii Secundi Epist. Lib. I. Epist. XXIV.

'Tis Suetonius' country this; and he
Near Tibur raised his humble villa where
Some vine-clad wall the years still kindly spare,
And arcade's ruin wreathed in greenery.

Here, far from Rome, he came each fall to see
The softest, deepest blue the heavens can wear,
And elms to harvest of their vintage cheer.
His life flowed on in calm tranquillity.

To this sweet pastoral peace would Claudius come,
Caligula and Nero; here would roam
Vile Messalina in her purple stoled;

And here with pointed stylus he has told,
Scratched in the unpitying wax, the horror's sum
Of him who Capri fouled when he was old.

LUPERCUS

M. Val. Martialis.   Lib. I, Epigr. CXVIII.

Thus Lupercus, soon as he sees me:—Poet dear,
Of Latin's best new Epigram of thine;—
To have me send my slave, dost not incline,
For loan of all thy works, when morrow's here?

—Ah, no. He limps, he pants, he's old and sere,
My stairs are steep, thy house remote from mine;
Dost thou not live close by the Palatine?
Atrectus in the Argiletum's near.

His shop is on the Forum. He sells cheap
The tomes of dead and living; Virgil he does keep,
Terence and Pliny, Silius, Phædrus and the rest;

There, on a shelf, and one not very high,
Pounced, robed in purple, and in cedar nest,
Martial's for sale at five denarii.

THE TREBIA

This direful day dawn comes with fatal speed.
The camp has roused. Harsh rolls the river's course
Below, where water the Numidian horse;
And everywhere the pealing trumpets plead.

For spite of Scipio, of the augurs' rede,
Of Trebia's rage, of wind and rain adverse,
Sempronius, vain new glories to rehearse,
Has bade his lictors with the axe proceed.

The homes of Insubres the flames ensnare,
The horizon reddening with their gloomy glare;
And some have heard an elephant's far cry.

Beneath the bridge, leaning against an arch,
The pensive Hannibal, with triumph high,
Lists to the tramping legions as they march.

AFTER CANNÆ

One consul killed, the other toward Liternum fled
Or toward Venusia. Aufidus choked full
With dead and arms. Lightning has struck the capitol;
The bronze sweats, and wan are the heavens red.

In vain High Pontiff has a lectisternium led,
And twice consulted sibyl's oracle;
The sob of father, widow, orphan, knows no lull,
Till Rome with grief and terror bows her head.

Each evening to the aqueducts they swarm:
Plebs, slaves, the women, children, the deform,
All that Suburra or ergastulum can spew,

To see, on Sabine Mount of blood-hued dyes,
Seated on elephant Gætulian, rise
The one-eyed Chieftain to their anxious view.

TO A TRIUMPHER

Illustrious Imperator, thine arch crown
With old chiefs yoked, barbarian warriors' throng,
Bits that to armor and to ships belong,
And captive fleet with stern and rostrum shown.

Whoe'er thou art, from Ancus sprung or clown,
Thy honors, names and family, short or long,
In bas-relief and frieze engrave them strong,
For fear the future dim thy just renown.

Even now Time lifts his fatal arm. Dost hope
To give thy fame's report eternal scope?
Why, let an ivy climb, thy trophy dies;

And on the scattered blocks thy deeds did vaunt,
Where choked with grass thy glory's ruin lies,
Some Samnite mower will his scythe make blunt.

ANTONY AND CLEOPATRA

THE CYDNUS

Beneath triumphal blue of flaming ray
The waves the barge's glittering silver know,
And perfumes in its track from censers flow,
Where rustle silks, and flutes mellifluous play.

Content not on her royal dais to stay,
Cleopatra seeks the gorgeous, hawk-decked prow,
Where, peering out, in evening's splendid glow
She seems great golden bird in watch for prey.

At Tarsus see the warrior now disarmed:
The Lagidus opes wide, in air all charmed,
Her amber arms where purple blends with rose;

And she has not seen near, as fateful sign,
Shedding the rose leaves on the water, those
Twin ones, Desire and Death, that are divine.

EVENING OF BATTLE

Severe the battle's shock. Centurions
And tribunes, rallying their men, drink in
Once more from air that vibrates with their din
The scents and ardors of red slaughter's sons.

With gloomy eyes, computing their lost ones,
The soldiers see, like leaves of autumn's kin,
Afar, Phraortes' archers whirl and spin;
And sweat adown their tawny faces runs.

And then appeared, with arrows bristling round,
Red from the vermeil stream of many a wound,
'Neath floating purple and the brass's glare,

To sound of trumpets' flourish, grand of mien,
Quelling his plunging horse, and bathed in sheen
Of fiery sky, the Imperator there.

ANTONY AND CLEOPATRA

On Egypt sleeping under sky of brass
The twain gazed wistfully from terrace high,
And watched the Flood, through Delta rolling nigh,
Toward Saïs or Bubastis slowly pass.

The Roman felt beneath his thick cuirass—
Like captive soldier stilling infant's cry—
On his triumphant bosom swooning lie
Her form voluptuous in his close embrace.

Turning her pallid head between his arms
Toward him made mad by perfume's conquering charms,
She raised her mouth and crystalline, fond eye;

And o'er her bent, the Chieftain did behold
In her great orbs, starry with dots of gold,
Only a boundless sea where galleys fly.

EPIGRAPHIC SONNETS

Bagneres-de-Luchon, Sept. 188..

THE VOW

<table>
<tr><td>ILIXONI
DEO
FAB. FESTA
V. S. L. M.</td><td>ISCITTO DEO
HVNNV
VLOHOXIS
FIL.
V. S. L. M.</td></tr>
</table>

Of old, Iberus, Gall with flaxen mane,
And the Garumnus brown, with colors bold
On votive marble cut by them, have told
The water's excellence and power o'er bane.

Beneath Venasque bald the Emperors then
Built pool and thermæ of the Roman mould,
And Fabia Festa, like the others controlled,
Has given the Gods the mallow and vervaine.

As when Ilixon and Iscitt were young,
The springs their song divine to me have sung,
Where in moraine's pure air the sulphur still fumes on.

Hence in this vow-sworn verse I fain would see,
As Hunnu, son of Ulohox, did formerly,
The Subterranean Nymphs barbaric altar own.

THE SPRING

NYMPHIS AVG. SACRVM.

'Neath brier and grass the altar buried lies,
And falling drop by drop the nameless spring
Fills the lone vale with plaintive murmuring.
'Tis Nymph who weeps oblivion's miseries.

The useless mirror which no ripple plies
The dove but seldom kisses with her wing,
And there the moon, in dark sky hovering,
Her pallid visage still alone espies.

At times a herdsman pauses there a space
To drink, and on the antique flagstone then
Pours from his hand the leavings that remain.

Unwitting he has done as all his race,
For he on Roman cippus has not seen
The patera anear libation's vase.

THE BEECH-TREE GOD

FAGO DEO.

The house of the Garumnus glads the ground
Beneath a torso-muscled beech where wells
A God's pure sap by which the white bark swells.
The mother forest makes his utmost bound;

For by the seasons blest he there has found
Nuts, wood and shade, and creatures that he fells
With bow and spear, or with sly lures compels,
For flesh to eat or fleece to wrap him round.

Long has he lived, rich, happy, freest of the free;
And when at eve he home returns, the Tree
With arms familiar gives him welcome's good.

And at the last when death shall lay him low,
His grandsons shall cut out his coffin's wood
From heart corruptless of the worthiest bough.

TO THE DIVINE MOUNTAINS.

GEMINVS SERVVS

ET PRO SVIS CONSERVIS.

Blue glaciers, peaks of marble, granite, slate,
Moraines whence winds from Bègle to Néthou
The wheat and rye send blighting ruin through,
Lakes, woods of shade and nest, steep crags serrate;

Dark vales and caves—the ancient exile's fate,
Who ne'er submitting to the tyrant crew,
The chamois, bear, the wolf, and eagle knew—
Abysses, torrents, cliffs, blest be your state!

From the harsh town and prison having flown,
Thy twin slave to the Mountains rears this stone—
The sacred guard of liberty to be;

And on these silence-pulsing summits clear,
In the all-boundless air so pure and free,
I trust a freeman's cry again to hear!

THE EXILED

MONTIBVS...
GARRI DEO...
SABINVLA.
V. S. L. M.

In this wild vale where Cæsar bids thee sigh,
Upon a moss-grown rock on Ardiège road,
With bended silvered head too early snowed,
Slowly each eve thou comest there to lie.

Thy youth, thy villa, greet again thine eye,
And Flamen red, as when with train he strode;
And so to ease thy longing's heavy load,
Sad Sabinula, thou regard'st the sky.

Toward seven-pointed Gar all dazzling bright,
The homing eagles in belated flight
Carry the dreams forever in thy mind;

And lonely, desireless, nought from man to come,
Thou raisest altars to the Mountains kind,
Whose Gods the nearest solace thee from Rome.

THE MIDDLE AGE AND THE RENAISSANCE

CHURCH WINDOW

This window has seen dames and lords of might,
Sparkling with gold, with azure, flame and nacre,
Bow down, before the altar of their Maker,
The pride of crest and hood to august right;

Whene'er to horn's or clarion's sound, with tight
Held sword in hand, gerfalcon or the saker,
Toward plain or wood, Byzantium or Acre,
They started for crusade or herons' flight.

Today, the seigniors near their chatelaines,
With hound low crouching at their long poulaines,
Extended lie upon the marble floor.

All still are they, voiceless and deaf; while e'er
They gaze, with stony eyes that ne'er see more,
On window's rose blooming forever there.

EPIPHANY

Then, Balthazar, Melchior, Gaspar—Magian Kings,
Laden with vases where enamels glow,
Vermeil and silver, with their camels go,
As in the bodied, old imaginings.

From the far East they bear their offerings
To feet of God's son, born to suage the woe
Of man and beast that suffer here below.
Their robes beflowered a page upbearing brings.

At stable's theshold where waits Joseph mild,
With chieftain's crown they low salute the Child,
Who laughs and eyes them with admiring cheer.

'Tis thus that when Augustus ruled, from far
There came, presenting incense, gold and myrrh,
The Magian Kings, Gaspar, Melchior and Balthazar.

THE WOOD-WORKER OF NAZARETH

A table to complete, the master wood-worker
Has bent o'er board since dawn, with weary strain,
Handling by turns the chisel and the plane,
The grating rasp and smoothing polisher.

With pleasure hence he sees, toward evening, near
The lengthening shadow of the great platane,
Where Virgin and her mother holy Anne,
With Jesus nigh them, go for restful cheer.

The parching air stirs not the leaves at all;
And Joseph, sore fatigued, his gouge lets fall,
As with his apron he would dry his face;

But the divine Apprentice, in a glory's fold,
Makes alway, in the shop's obscurest place,
Fly from the cutting edge his chips of gold.

MEDAL

Seignior of Rimini, Vicar and Podestate:
His hawk face lives, confessed here or withdrawn
In bronze dim glimmering as the gray of dawn,
In orb Matteo de' Pastis did create.

Of all the tyrants whom a people hate,
Count, Marquis, Duke, Prince, Princeling, there is none,
Though Can's, Galeas', Hercules', or Ezzelin's name he own,
The Malatesta in their pride can mate.

This one, the best, this Sigismond Pandolf,
To kindred gives Romagna, Marches and the Gulf,
A temple builds, makes love and sings the while;

And even their women stern and rude are shown,
For on the selfsame bronze that sees Isotta smile
The Elephant triumphal tramps the primrose down.

THE RAPIER

On pommel's gold Calixtus Pope we read.
The trammel, barque, tiara and the keys,
Adorn with raised and sumptuous blazonries
The guard where Borgian ox is armoried.

There laughs, midst ivy gemmed with coral seed,
In fusil, Faunus or Priapus. These,
With the enameled metal's fulgencies,
Make rapier, more than Pope, our wonder feed.

Master Antonio Perez de Las Cellas planned
This pastoral staff for the first Borgia's hand,
As if his famous lineage he had foretold;

And more than Ariosto or than Sannazar,
It tells, through blade of steel and hilt of gold,
Of Pontiff Alexander and the Prince Cæsar.

AFTER PETRARCH

As you came out of church, all piously
Your noble hands bestowed alms freely there,
And in the darkened porch you shone so fair,
The poor all heaven's riches seemed to see.

I then saluted you most graciously,
Humbly, as suits one in discretion's care,
When, drawing close your robe, with angry air
You covered up your eyes and turned from me.

But Love, that will the most rebellious rule,
Would not permit, less kind than beautiful,
That pity's source all mercy should refuse;

And in your veiling you were then so slow,
That your umbrageous lashes throbbed as does
Dark leafage under filtering starlight's glow.

ON THE BOOK OF LOVES
OF PIERRE DE RONSARD

In Bourgueil Gardens more than one of yore
Engraved loved names on bark with heavy stroke,
And many a heart 'neath Louvre's gold ceilings shook,
At flash of smile, with pride to very core.

What matters it?—their joy or grief e'ermore
Is stilled; they lie between four boards of oak,
Where under grass-grown cover nought has woke
Their torpid dust that feeds oblivion's shore.

All die. Mary, Helen, and thee, Cassandra, all
Your lovely forms to lifeless ashes fall,
—Nor rose nor lily sees the morrow's land—

Still, Ronsard by the Seine and Loire has wove
For brows of ours, with an immortal hand,
Fame's laurel leaf with myrtle leaf of Love.

THE BEAUTIFUL VIOLE

To Henry Cros
A vous trouppe légère
Qui d'aile passagère
Par le monde volez...
JOACHIM DU BELLAY.

On balcony leaned, where one the road that lies
From banks of Loire to Italy may trace,
Beneath pale olive branch she bows her face.
The violet blooms today, tomorrow dies.

Her viol then with fragile hand she tries,
That soothes her solitude and saddened case,
And revery flies to him who for a space
Forgets her as he walks 'neath Roman skies.

Of her he called his darling Angevine
The vibrant strings are stirred by spirit divine,
Whene'er her troubled heart feels love's sharp pain;

And given to winds her voice is borne far on,
Caressing, it may be, the faithless one,
In song he sang for winnower of grain.

EPITAPH

After the verses of Henry III.

O passing one, 'tis Hyacinthe lies here,
Who, living, Maugiron's seignior was; he's gone—
May God enfold him and his sins condone!
In field he fell, and holy ground's his fare.

Not one, not Quelús even, in pearl-gemmed gear,
Plumed cap or plaited ruff, the better shone;
And so thou seest, by a new Myron done,
This funeral stone a branch of jacinth wear.

King Henry kissed and clipped him and his shroud
Put on; then willed that to Saint-Germain should
Be borne his pale, cold form of matchless grace;

And anxious grief like his might never die,
He raised this emblem in this sacred place—
Sad, sweet memorial of Apollo's sigh.

GILDED VELLUM

The gold, old Master Binder, thou didst chase
On the book's back and in the edge's grain,
Despite the irons pushed with free-hand main,
In vivid, brilliant hue no more we trace.

The figures which so deftly interlace
Grow daily on the fine, white skin less plain;
And scarce we see the ivy thou didst train
To wind in beauty o'er the cover's space.

But this translucent, supple ivory,
Marguerite, Marie—Diane, it even may be,
With loving fingers have of old caressed;

And this paled vellum Clovis Eve gilt seems
To evoke, I know not by what charm possessed,
Their perfume's spirit and shadow of their dreams.

THE DOGARESSA

On porticos of marble palace these
Seigniors converse who live through Titian's lore,
And whose great collars, weighing marc or more,
Enhance their red dalmatic draperies.

With eyes where shine patrician dignities,
The old lagoons they look serenely o'er,
Beneath clear skies of Venice, to the shore
And sparkling azure of the Adrian seas.

And whilst the swarm of brilliant Cavaliers
Trail gold and purple by the white stone stairs,
Bathed in the luminous blue with merry vein;

Indolent, superb, a Dame, retired in shade,
Turning half round in billows of brocade,
Smiles at the negro boy who bears her train.

ON THE OLD-BRIDGE

Antonio di Sandro orefice.

The Master Goldsmith has, since matins, where
Enamel sparkling from his pencils flowed,
On nielloed pax and gold fermail bestowed
His Latin mottoes in florescence rare.

On Bridge whose bells with music filled the air,
Camail and frock were by the cape elbowed;
And sun, upmounting in a heaven that glowed,
Set nimbus bright on Florentines the fair.

Then caught in dream 'twere useless to oppose,
The pensive novices forgot to close
The hands of the betrothed on ring's chaton;

Whilst with a tempered burin like stylet,
The young Cellini, nothing seeing, set
The Titan's combat dagger's pommel on.

THE OLD GOLDSMITH

Than any master the maitrise can blaze,
E'en Ruyz, Arphé, Ximeniz, Becerrill,
I've deftlier set the ruby, pearl, beryl,
Curved vase's handle, wrought its hammered frieze.

In silver, on the enamel's irised glaze,
I've carved and painted, risking soul the while,
Instead of Christ on cross and saint on grill,
Shame! Bacchus drunk or Danaë's amaze.

The rapier's iron I've damaskeened full well,
And, for vain boastings of these works of hell,
Adventured the eternal part of me;

And so, as now my years toward evening fly,
O would, as did Fray Juan de Ségovie,
While chasing gold of monstrance I might die.

THE SWORD.

Believe me, pious child, take the old road.
This sword of straight quillons entwisted thus,
In hand of one both quick and vigorous,
Weighs not so much as Roman ritual's load.

The Hercules thou hold'st in lukewarm mode,
Its torso polished by thy grandsires' use,
Now swells beneath its surface splendorous
The iron muscles that proclaim a God.

Try it. The supple steel a bouquet shows
Of sparks. The solid blade is one of those
To send a prideful shiver through the breast;

Bearing, in hollow of its brilliant gorge,
Like noble Dame a gem, the stamp impressed
Of Julian del Rey, prince of the forge.

TO CLAUDIUS POPELIN

On fragile glass within the lead's embrace
Old masters painted lords of high degree
Turning their chaperons in piety,
And humbly bent in prayer as bourgeois race.

The breviary's vellum others did grace
With saints and ornaments a joy to see,
Or made to glow, by pliant touch and free,
Gold arabesques on ewer's bellied space.

Today, Claudius, their rival and their son,
Reviving in himself their works sublime,
Has fixed his genius solid metal on;

And so, beneath the enamel of my rhyme,
I would keep green, upon his brow alway,
For future ages, the heroic Bay.

ENAMEL

The furnace glows for plaque. Thy lamp take now;
Model paillon where colors quickly run,
And fix with fire in the pigment dun
The sparkling powder which thy pencils know.

Wilt wreathe with myrtle or with bay the brow
Of thinker, hero, prince, or lover lone?
Near what God wilt, black firmament upon,
Scaled hydra or gray hippocampus show?

No. Let the sapphire-sparkling orb reveal
From Ophir's warrior race some proud profile—
Thalestris, Auda, Bradamant, Penthesilea.

And that her beauty may be still more fell,
Casque her blonde locks with wingèd beast, and be a
Gorgon of gold on bosom's lovely swell.

DREAMS OF ENAMEL

In sombre room where roars the athanor
The brick-imprisoned fire burns glowingly,
And by enamel's sorcery will be
Richer than gold the copper evermore.

Beneath my brushes are born, live, run and soar,
The monstrous people of mythology:
Pan, Centaurs, Sphinx, Chimæra, the Orgy,
And race of Gorgo, Pegasus and Chrysaor.

Shall I now paint Achilles weeping near
Penthesilea? Orpheus, with arms toward banished dear
For whom the infernal gate shall ne'er relent?

Hercules confounding the Avernian hound,
Or Virgin at the cavern's outer bound
With writhing body which the Dragons scent?

THE CONQUERORS

THE CONQUERORS

As falcons from their native eyry soar,
So, tired with weight of their disdainful woes,
Rovers and captains out of Palos rose,
To daring, brutish dreams mad to the core.

They longed to seize the fabled metal ore
Which in Cipango's mines to ripeness grows,
And trade-winds willingly inclined their prows
Toward the mysterious occidental shore.

Each eve, athirst for morrow's epic scene,
The tropic sea with phosphorescent sheen
Bound all their visions in mirage of gold;

Or from the fore-deck of their white carvels,
They watched amazed on alien skies enscrolled
Strange stars new risen from ocean's glowing wells.

YOUTH

Juan Ponce de Leon, by the Devil led,
With years weighed down and crammed with antique lore,
Seeing age blanch his stubby locks still more,
The far seas scoured to find Health's Fountain-head.

Haunted by fruitless dream his vessels sped
Three years the glaucous solitudes to explore,
Until, heart-sickening the Bermudan shore,
Beneath Floridian skies enchantments spread.

Then the Conquistador his madness blessed,
And with enfeebled hand his pennon pressed
In that bright earth which opened for his tomb.

Old man, most happy thou: thy fortune sooth
Is deathlike, but thy dream bears beauty's bloom,
For Fame has given thee immortal Youth.

TOMB OF THE CONQUEROR

Where the catalpa's arches spread their shade,
Where tulip tree in petaled glory blows,
He found not in the fatal earth repose;
His victor step in Florida ne'er stayed.

For such as he no paltry tomb be made;
The conqueror of Western India shows
His winding sheet where Mississippi flows.
Nor Redskins nor gray bears his rest invade.

He sleeps where virgin waters carved his couch;
What matters monument, the taper's vouch,
The psalm, the chapel and the offering?

Since northern winds, amidst the cypress' sighs,
Eternal prayers forever weep and sing
O'er the Great River where de Soto lies.

IN THE TIME OF CHARLES FIFTH, EMPEROR

We count him with the great who've passed away,
For 'twas his daring keel that first was seen
To thread the isles of Gardens of the Queen,
Where breezes sweet with perfume ceaseless play.

Far more than years, the surge and biting spray,
Storms, and the long, long calms between,
Love of the mermaid and the fright, I ween,
Blanched his brown hair and turned his beard to gray.

Through him Castile has grandly triumphed, since
His fleet the peerless empire made complete,
Wherefrom the circling sun might ne'er retreat.

Such is Bartholomew Ruiz, the prince
Of pilots, who, on royal shield enscrolled,
Bears sable anchor, with the cable, gold.

THE ANCESTOR

To Claudius Popelin.

Through these deep wrinkles glory's plough has made
The hardy features of this Cavalier,
Whose face proclaims that nought has made him fear
The heat of torrid sun or battle's blade.

Where'er his foot was he the cross displayed—
Côte-Ferme, the islands, or sierras drear;
And Andes crossed, he took his pennon where
The gulf's mad waves the Floridas invade.

Mid splendid foliage in his bronzèd mail,
Through pencil thine his last descendants hail
Again their melancholic, proud grandsire;

His gloomy eyes in search, as once of old,
In the enameled sky's all lustrous fire,
Of dazzling visions of **Castile** of Gold.

TO A FOUNDER OF A CITY

Weary with seeking Ophir's shadowy strand,
Thou foundedst, where these waves each sense enchant,
And where thou didst the royal standard plant,
A modern Carthage for the fabled land.

Thou wouldst not have thy name fore'er unscanned,
And thoughtst to have it evermore all blent
With thy dear city's blood-immixed cement;
But thy hope, soldier, rested on the sand.

For Cartagena, choked with torrid breath,
And robed in gloom, beholds thy wall meet death
In ocean's shore-devouring, feverous stream;

And on thy crest but shines, O Conqueror bold,
As proof heraldic of thy splendid dream,
A silver city under palm of gold.

TO THE SAME

Their Inca, Aztec, Yaquis, let them flaunt;
Their Andes, forest, river or their plain--
These men of whom no marks or proofs remain
Save titled name of Marquis or of Count.

But thou didst found—boast that my race can vaunt—
A modern Carthage in the Carib main,
And Magdalena even to Darien
Where flows Atrato, saw the cross high mount.

Upon thine isle where waves their breakers hurl,
Despite the wind's, bolt's, man's, the centuries' raids,
Her forts and convents still their stoutness hold;

Hence thy last sons, no trefoil, ache or pearl,
Stamp on their shield, but palm which overshades
A silver city with its plume of gold.

TO A DEAD CITY

Cartagena de Indias
1532—1583—1697.

City deject, the Queen whom seas obeyed!
Unhindered now the shark pursues its prey,
And clouds alone in lengthening shadows play,
Where once the giant galleons were arrayed.

Since Drake was here, since faithless Briton's raid,
Thy broken walls have crumbled to decay,
And like a necklace gemmed with black pearls aye
Appear the rents by Pointis' bullets made.

Between the burning sky and foaming sea,
When drowseful noontide's sun bids sleep to be,
Thou dream'st, O Warrior, of thy conquering men;

And in the languorous evenings warm and calm,
Cradling thy glory lost, thou sleepest then
To long-drawn music of the quivering palm.

THE ORIENT AND TROPICS

VISION OF KHEM

I

Midday. The air burns, and under blazing sky
The languid river rolls in leaden flight;
From blinding zenith falls the arrowy light,
And Phre all Egypt rules implacably.

The sphinxes with ne'er drooping eyelids lie
Extended on their sand-bathed sides, with sight,
Mysterious and long, fixed on the white
Needles of stone inordinately high.

Nought stains or specks the heavens serene and clear
Save the far vultures in their endless sweep;
The flame immense lulls man and beast to sleep.

The parched soil crackles, and Anubis here,
Immobile midst this heated joy, barks on
With brazen throat in silence toward the sun.

II

The moon on Nilus sheds resplendent light;
And see, the old death-city stirs amain,
Where kings their hieratic pose maintain
In bandelette and funeral coating dight.

Countless as in the days of Ramses' might
The hosts all noiseless forming mystic train
(A multitude granitic dreams enchain)
With stately, ordered ranks, march in the night.

Leaving the hieroglyphic walls' display,
They follow Bari which the priests convey,
Of Ammon-Ra, who holds the sun at will;

And sphinxes, and the rams with disk vermeil,
Uprise at once in wild amaze as they
Break with a start from sleep's eternal seal.

And the crowd grows, increasing more and more:
Empty the hypogeum with beds of night,
And from cartouche the sacred hawks in flight
Midst the great host in freedom proudly soar.

Beasts, peoples, kings, they go. Fierce foreheads o'er,
The gold uræus curls with sparkling light,
But thick bitumen seals their thin lips tight.
At head, the Gods: Hor, Knoum, Ptah, Neith, Hathor;

Next, those whom Ibis-headed Thoth controls,
In shenti robed and crowned with pshent all decked
With lotus blue. The pomp triumphant rolls

Midst the horrific gloom of temples wrecked,
While the cold pavements wrapped in moonlit air
Show giant shadows strangely lengthened there.

THE PRISONER

To Gérôme.

Muezzins' calls have ceased. The greenish sky
Is fringed with gold and purple in the west;
The crocodile now dives to muddy rest,
And hushed to stillness is the Flood's last cry.

On crossed legs smoker wise, with dreamy eye,
The Chief sits mute, by haschisch fumes oppressed,
While on the gangia's rowing bench with zest
Their bending oars two naked negroes ply.

In stern, jocund and mouthing insults there,
Scraping harsh guzla to a savage air,
An Arnaut bends, with brutal look and vile;

For bound to boat and bleeding from his cords,
An old Sheik gravely, stupidly regards
The minarets that tremble in the Nile.

THE SAMURAI

This was a man with two swords.

On biwa's strings a finger light she throws,
As through the latticed bamboo she espies,
Where the flat shore in dazzling radiance lies,
The victor whom her love in dreaming knows.

'Tis he. Engirt with swords, fan-decked, he goes.
The tasseled girdle steeped in scarlet dyes
Cuts his dark armor, and the blazonries
Of Tokugawa or Hizen his shoulder shows.

This handsome warrior in his dress of plate,
Of brilliant lacquers, bronze and silk, would mate
Some black crustacean, gigantesque, vermeil.

He sees her;—and he smiles behind his mask,
While his more rapid pace makes brighter still
The two gold horns which tremble on his casque.

THE DAIMIO

Morning of battle.

Under black war-whip that four pompons has,
The martial, neighing stallion prances high,
And with the clank of sabre rattlings fly
From metal-plated skirt and bronze cuirass.

The Chief, in lacquer dressed, crepon and brass,
Takes hairy mask from his smooth face to spy
Nippon's aurora light vermilion sky
On which volcano lifts its snowy mass.

But in the gold-hued east the star's bright ray,
Lighting in glory this disastrous day,
He sees above the sea resplendent glow;

To shield his eyes that would no terror shun,
His iron fan he opens with a blow,
Its satin blazing with a crimson sun.

FLOWERS OF FIRE

In ages past since Chaos' mighty throes,
The flame in torrents from this crater flowed,
And its plumed fire in lonely grandeur glowed
At loftier height than Chimborazo's snows.

The summit echoless no murmur knows;
The bird now drinks where cinders poured their flood;
And bound in Earth's congealèd lava-blood
The soil has found inviolate repose.

Yet—act supreme of fire in time of old—
In orle of crater's mouth forever cold,
Shedding o'er comminuted rocks its light,

Like peal of thunder in the silence rolled,
Standing in pollen dust of powdered gold,
The flame-born cactus spreads its petals bright.

CENTURY FLOWER

On topmost point of calcined rocky steeps,
Where the volcanic flux dried up of yore,
The seeds which winds from Gualatieri bore
Sprout, and the holding plant in frailness creeps.

It lives. Its roots dip down to darkness' deeps,
And light gives nourishment from out its store,
Till a century's suns have ripened more and more
The large-grown bud whose stalk it proudly tips.

At last, in air which burns it as of old,
With giant pistil raised, it bursts, when lo!
The stamen darts afar the pollen's gold;

And the great aloe with its scarlet blow,
Has lived, for love-dreamt hymen's joys unknown,
One hundred years to bear this blossom lone.

CORAL REEF

The sun beneath the sea, mysterious dawn,
Illumes the depths where coral forests spread,
And where immix in tepid basin's bed
The living plants with creatures flower-like blown.

All those that iodine's or salt's tint own,
Anemones, urchins, mosses and sea-weed,
Cover, with purple-colored, sumptuous brede,
The madrepore's vermiculate, pale stone.

With splendid scale that all enamels dims
A monstrous fish across the branches swims.
In the pellucid shade he indolently prowls;

When, at quick stroke of his bright-flaming fin,
Through the immobile, crystal blue a sheen
Of emerald, gold and nacre shivering rolls.

NATURE AND DREAM

ANTIQUE MEDAL

In gold and purple Ætna robes the vine
Which gave Theocritus antique Erigone;
But those fair ones who graced his poesy
No more on earth today show living sign.

Losing the pure from her profile divine,
Arethusa, who by turns was bond and free,
Mixed in her Grecian blood whate'er could be
Of Saracen rage with pride of Anjou's line.

Time goes. All die. Even marble feels death's dews.
Agrigentum's but a shade, and Syracuse
Sleeps under shroud of her indulgent sky;

And nought but love-wrought metal undecayed,
On silver medals, guards in flower the high,
Immortal beauty of Sicilian maid.

FUNERAL

When ancient warriors to Hades went,
Their sacred image Greece attended where
Illustrious Phocis did her temples rear
O'er Pytho wreathed with lightnings never spent.

Their Shades, when evening's starry rain is sprent
On radiant islands and on gulfs austere,
From headlands' shining heights the chanting hear
Of Salamis above their tombs lament.

But I shall feel when old grief's cureless wound;
My body will be nailed in coffin's bound,
With cost of earth, of priest and tapers duly paid.

And yet, I've dreamed the glorious destiny mine
Of sinking in the sun as sires divine,
Still young and wept by hero and by maid.

VINTAGE

The wearied vintagers have broken their lines,
With voices ringing in eve's vibrant air,
And as the women toward the wine-press fare,
They blend with song appealing cries and signs.

All white with flight of swans the heaven shines
As when in Naxos' isle, fuming like censer rare,
The Bacchanal saw the Cretan seated where
The beauteous Tamer thrilled with blood of vines.

Today, the radiant thyrsus brandishing,
Dionysus, Gods and beasts all conquering,
No more the wreathèd yoke on panther ties;

But sun's child Autumn twines, as once of old,
With sanguined pampre of the antique mysteries
The black chevelure and crinière of gold.

SIESTA

No sound of insect or marauding bee;
All sleep in shade of wood o'erpowered by sun,
Whose light through foliage strained falls softly on
The emerald moss with bosom velvety.

Sifting the dome obscure, bright Noon roams free,
And o'er my lashes half with sleep foredone
Bids myriad lacing lightnings furtive run,
That in the warm shade cross in lengthening tracery.

Toward gauze of fire the rays weave hies
The fragile swarm of gorgeous butterflies,
Mad with sap's perfume and the luminous beams.

My trembling fingers on each thread are set,
And in gold meshes of this subtile net,
Harmonious hunter, I imprison my dreams.

THE SEA OF BRITTANY

To Emmanuel Lansyer.

A PAINTER

He knows the ancient, pensive race of dry
And flinty Breton soil—unvaried plain
Of rose and gray, where yew and ivy reign
O'er crumbling manors which beneath them lie.

From wind-swept slopes of writhing beech his eye
Has joyed to see bleak autumn's stormful train
Whelm crimson sun in the tempestuous main;
His lips all salt with spray from reefs dashed high.

He paints the ocean, splendid, vast and sad,
With cloud in amethystine beauty clad,
In foaming emerald and calm sapphire;

And water, air, shade, hour, which undiscerned would fly,
Fixing on canvas, he has made respire
In the sand's mirror the occidental sky.

BRITTANY

That joyous blood the sullen mind may quell,
The lungs should deeply drink the Atlantic air
Perfumed with wrack the sea delights to bear.
Arvor gives capes by surge besprinkled well,

And heather and furze in blossomy glory swell.
The land of demons, dwarfs, and clans that were,
Friend, on the mountain's granite guard with care—
Immobile man near thing immutable.

Come. Everywhere on moors about Arèz
Mounts toward heaven—cypress no hand can slay—
The menhir raised o'er ashes of the Brave;

And Ocean, that beds with algæ's golden store
Voluptuous Is and mighty Occismor,
Shall soothe thy sadness in his cradling wave.

FLOWERY SEA

O'er variegated plain the harvest flows,
Rolls, undulates and breaks with wind rocked high,
And harrow's profile on the distant sky
Is like tossed boat whose bowsprit blackly shows.

Beneath my feet to west's deep purple glows
Cerulean, violet or rosy dye,
With white of sheep the ebb makes scattering fly
On sea where meadow infinitely grows.

The gulls that follow where the tide is rolled,
Toward ripened grain which swells in billow's gold,
In wingèd whirling speed with joyous cries;

While from the land a honey-laden breeze
Dispersed, made mad with wildering ecstacies,
On flowery ocean, swarms of butterflies.

SUNSET

The furze in granite set with golden store
Gilds heights by west illumined; and afar,
Shining still brilliant at its foaming bar,
The endless sea begins where ends the shore.

Night, silence, are at my feet. Quiet broods o'er
The nest; 'neath smoking thatch man rests from care;
And nought but Angelus mid misty air
Unites its voice with ocean's vasty roar.

Then, as from bottom of abyss, there rise
From trails, ravines and moors the distant cries
Of tardy herdsmen who their kine constrain.

In shade the horizon is completely bound,
And dying sun on rich and sombre ground
Shuts the gold branches of his crimson fan.

STAR OF THE SEA

With linen coifs, arms crossed on breast, and dight
In coarsest woollen or in thin percale,
The women kneel on rock of slip while all
Regard the Isle of Batz by sea made white.

Their fathers, husbands, lovers, sons, unite
With those of Paimpol, Audierne and Cancale,
To sail for distant North. How many shall,
Of these bold fishers, see no more home's light!

Above the noise of ocean and the shore
The plaintive chant ascends as they implore
The holy Star—sailors' last hope in ill;

And Angelus, each swarthy face in prayerful wise,
From belfries of Roscoff to those of Sybiril
In pallid, roseate sky, flies, tolls and dies.

THE BATH

Like handsome antique monster, man and beast,
Bitless and free, the sea have entered in,
Midst the gold mist of acrid pulverin—
On fiery sky athletic group expressed.

The savage horse and rustic tamer with zest
Inhale the salty fragrance as with keen,
Abandoned joy their naked flesh and skin
Are by Atlantic's icy stream caressed.

The surge swells, runs, wall-like is piled,
Then breaks. They cry. His tail the stallion plies
Till azure wave in jets transplendent flies;

And with disheveled locks and aspect wild
Their smoking breasts in passion they oppose
To foaming billows' lashing, angry blows.

CELESTIAL BLAZON

I've seen, with blue the enamel would attest,
By purple, silvery clouds, and coppery,
In Occident the eye was dazzled to see,
On heavenly window blazon's wealth impressed.

For crest and bearers, some heraldic beast,
The unicorn, leopard, allerion or guivré—
Monsters, captive giants a breeze might free—
Displayed its figure and upraised its breast.

In those strange combats in the fields of space,
In which the Archangels vanquished Seraphs base,
Sure, Baron gained this shield so heavenly;

It bears, like those which seized Constantinople,
In proper cross, Michæl or George maybe,
The sun, bezant of gold, on sea sinople.

ARMOR

For guide to Raz a shepherd at Trogor,
Haired like Évhage of old, took me in care;
And then we trod, breathing its spicy air,
The Cymric land with golden broom grown o'er.

The west grew red, and still we walked yet more,
Till to my face the brine its breath did bear;
When cried the man, stretching his long arm where
The landscape lay beyond: Sell euz ar·mor!

And o'er the heather's rose the ocean was seen,
Which, splendid, monstrous, waters with the green
Salt of its waves the cape's granitic breast;

Then thrilled my heart, before the horizon lined
On ever deepening shadow of the west,
With joys of space and of the dauntless wind.

RISING SEA

The sun a beacon seems with fixed, white light.
From Raz far as Penmarc'h the coast's in fume,
And only gulls across the storm and spume
With ruffled feathers whirl in aimless flight.

One after other, with impetuous might,
The glaucous waves beneath their mane of foam,
Dispersing clouds of mist to thunderous boom,
With plumes the distant, streaming reefs bedight.

And so the billows of my thought have course—
Spent hopes and dreams, regrets for wasted force,
With nothing left but mocking memory.

Ocean has spoken in fraternal strain,
For the same clamor which impels the sea
Mounts to the Gods from man, forever vain.

SEA BREEZE

The winter has deflowered garden and heath;
Nought lives; and on the rock's unchanging gray,
Where the Atlantic's endless billows play,
The last pistil to petal clings in death.

And yet, these subtile scents the sea breeze hath
Blown me I know not—warm effluvia they
That bid my heart to mad delight give way;
Whence comes this strangely odoriferous breath?

Ah! now it is revealed:—'Tis from the west
Three thousand leagues, where the Antilles rest,
Beneath the occidental star, in swoon;

And on this Cymric wave-lashed reef today
I've breathed the air perfumed by flower blown
Of old in garden of America.

THE SHELL

In what cold seas, under what winters' reign,
—Who can e'er know, O nacreous, fragile Shell!—
Hast thou through current, wave and tidal swell,
In shallows and abysses restless lain?

Today thou hast, far from the ebbing main,
Soft bed in golden sand, 'neath sky to dwell.
Vain hope: full long and sad, within thy cell
Still ever sounds great ocean's mournful strain.

My soul sonorous prison-chamber lies,
And like thyself forever weeps and sighs
Refrain of ancient clamor to be free;

So from the heart-depths all too full of Her,
Deaf, slow, insensible, yet deathless e'er,
The stormy, distant murmur moans in me.

THE BED

Whether with serge becurtained or brocade,
Sad as a tomb or joyous as a nest,
'Tis there man's born, unites, lies peace-possessed,
Child, spouse, old man, old woman, wife or maid.

Wedding or funeral, with holy water sprayed
Under black crucifix or branch that's blest,
All there begins, all there finds final rest,
From life's first light to death's eternal shade.

Rude, humble and closed, or proud with canopy
In gold or vermeil done triumphantly,
Of cypress, maple, or of oaken block,

Blest he who fearless sleeps, with nought to chide,
In great paternal bed of honored stock,
Where all his own were born and all have died.

DEATH OF THE EAGLE

Although beyond the eternal snows, aspires
The vast-winged eagle still to loftier air,
That nearer to the sun in blue more clear
He may renew his eyeball's splendid ires.

He rises. Sparks in torrents he inspires.
Still up, in proud, calm flight, he glories where
The storm breeds lightnings in its inmost lair;
Whereat his wings are smit by their fierce fires.

With scream, in waterspout borne whirlingly,
Shriveled, sublimely tasting flame's last kiss,
He plunges to the fulgurant abyss.

Happy he who, for Fame or Liberty,
In strength's full pride and dream's enrapturing bliss
Dies such undaunted, dazzling death as this.

MORE BEYOND

Through lions' torrid country man has sped,
Through that of poisons' and of reptiles' bale,
And vexed the sea where nautilus bends to gale
Along the gilded way the galleons led.

But farther than the Stream by whirlpools fed,
Than Spitzbergs' woes, than wastes of snow and hail,
The warm, free polar wave bathes isles where sail
Has ne'er been seen nor tent been ever spread.

Depart! The insuperable ice I'll dare,
For my stout spirit would no longer bear
The facile fame of Conquerors of Gold.

I go. I long to mount the topmost promontory,
So that the ocean silences enfold
May feed my pride with murmuring of glory.

LIFE OF THE DEAD

To the poet Armand Silvestre.

When over us the cross its shadow throws,
Our frames enshrouded in the mould of night,
Thy body shall reflower in lily white,
And from my flesh be born the ensanguined rose.

And Death divine, thy verse in music knows,
With silence and oblivion to his flight,
In heavens shall show us, lulled with gentle might,
Enchanted route where strange, new stars repose.

And mounting to the sun, within his breast
Our spirits twain shall melt and be possessed
Of blessedness of everlasting fire;

But Fame, anointing friend and child of song,
Shall give us an eternal life among
The immortal Shades made kin by glorious **Lyre**.

TO THE TRAGEDIAN E. ROSSI

After a recitation from Dante.

Rossi, I've seen thee in black robe the lief,
Weak heart of sad Ophelia rudely break,
And, tiger mad with love and fury, seek
To choke thy sobs in fatal handkerchief;

Macbeth and Lear I've seen, and wept with grief
When thou, Italian lover best, didst speak
Thy kissful woe to tombèd Juliet's cheek;
Yet, once I found still greater in thy sheaf:

For then I tasted horror and joy sublime
Of hearing for the first the triple rhyme
Sound in thy golden voice its iron swell;

And, red from flames of the infernal pool,
I saw—and shook to bottom of my soul—
The living Dante chant his song of Hell.

MICHELANGELO

Haunted he was by torment tragical,
When in the Sistine where no fête he knew,
Lonely, his Sibyls and his Prophets grew,
And his Last Judgment on the sombre wall.

He heard the tear-drops unremitting fall
(Titan whose wish to highest summits flew)
Where Country, Glory, Love, defeatures rue;
And deemed that dreams are false, that death wins all.

And so, these Giants, bloodless, weary grown,
These Slaves bound ever to the unyielding stone,
How strangely twisted at his sovereign will;

While in the marbles where his great thoughts fare,
How courses with emotion's deathless thrill
The passion of a God imprisoned there!

ON A BROKEN MARBLE

Pious the moss to see no more the ground;
For from this wasted wood forever gone
Is virgin who the milk and wine poured on
The earth to beauteous name that marked the bound.

The ivy, hop, viburnum, which around
This ruin gather, all to them unknown
Whether 'twas Silvan, Pan, Hermes or Faun,
Its maimèd front their twining horns have found.

Behold! The ray, caressful as of old,
In its flat face has set two orbs of gold;
As though from lip, the vines bid laughter run;

And (mobile spell), wind murmuring blown,
The leaves, the wandering shadows and the sun,
Have turned to living God this broken stone.

NOTES

THE MAGICIAN (page 31).

Having written a note of inquiry to my friend Professor Jacob Cooper, D. D., D. C. L., of Rutgers College, New Jersey, in regard to this sonnet, he wrote me in reply a letter from which I give the following extract as an elucidatory note:

The Mysteries of Samothrace, and especially the questions relating to the personality of the Cabiri (most probably derived from the Arabic كَبِير Kabhir, kindred with the Persian *Guebre*) are the most perplexing and obscure of all subjects of Classical Antiquity. The Samothracian Mysteries were undoubtedly the precursors of the Eleusinian. The notices of them are scattered and apocryphal. Their Ritual was guarded more closely, if possible, than the Eleusinian. The latter are a very interesting, though difficult theme; but have left many scattered notices which can be interpreted by reading between the lines. They are said to have been founded about 1200 B. C., and they continued until nearly 400 A. D. Hence there is much literature which treats of them *obiter*, but nothing can be known authoritatively because no one ever divulged the secrets. The substance of this literature appeared in an article in the New Englander (volume for 1876), which brought under contribution nearly all that could be reached.

But the Samothracian Mysteries and the question Who were the Cabiri? are far more difficult to investigate. The most clear information about these mysterious personages—sometimes represented as gods, again as demi-gods, and then as a priestly order—is given in the Paris Scholia to Apollonius Rhodius, Book 1, Line 913. I translate from this: "Mnaseas says that the Cabiri, by whom persons are initiated into the Samothracian Mysteries, are three in number; viz. Axieron, Axiokersan and Axiokerson: that Axieron is Demeter, Axiokersan is Persephone, and Axiokerson is Aides, (Pluto). Others add also a fourth, Kasmilos, that is Hermes, as Dionysidorus relates." So much for the Cabiri.

The Eumolpidai were a priestly family, deriving their origin from a Pelasgian Thracian named Eumolpus—"The one with a good voice, or melody." This man founded, and was the Chief Priest in, the Samothracian Mysteries; and he, or a member of his family, migrated to Attica where he founded the Eleusinian Mysteries, and became their Chief Priest or Hierophant. The Eumolpidai exercised various Civil Functions, besides the Priestly Office. At the command of the people they cursed such offenders as were guilty of great crimes; and the curse pursued the culprit, wherever he might flee, with the direst consequences. The Eumolpidai were clothed with long, purple robes—hence "*manteaux sanglants*"—and they shook these robes against the threshold, i. e. the home, of those they cursed. This was a significant action among all ancient peoples—*vide* Nehemiah, the Prophet, Cap. V, v. 13—and is so among orientals to this day. The curse which the Eumolpid uttered was executed by the Furies, who are often called κύνες—dogs; and they track up and howl after the wretch; and never relent, however sick at heart and weary of foot, he may be.

Now for your matter specifically:

In an unknown Greek author, believed to be Aelian, and quoted in defining a word by Suidas in his Greek Lexicon—in Greek—we have an account of a young woman who was betrothed, under the most solemn circumstances in the presence and by the authority of the Divinity of the Cabiri. (Betrothals were a part of the duties of these mysterious Divinities, as is shown by a well known case, viz. of Olympias and Philip, the parents of Alexander the Great). This damsel, after the solemn betrothal, was deserted by her affianced husband. She, then, as I quote from Suidas' Lexicon, translating the passage:

"Beseeches the Cabiri to avenge her, and follow up (i. e. to pursue to destruction) the perjurer." This is undoubtedly the love lorn damsel who is the "Magicienne" of your French Poet.

Bearing all that has been said above in our minds, let us look at the passage you quote:

L'Eumolpide vengeur n'a point dans Samothrace,
Secoué vers le seuil les longs manteaux sanglants,
Et malgré moi, je fuis, le cœur las, les pieds lents.
J'entends les chiens sacrés qui hurlent sur ma trace.

Now I take the meaning to be:

"The Eumolpid avenger has not in Samothrace
Shaken his long bloody (purple) robes against the threshold,
Yet, in spite of myself, I flee with sinking heart, and sluggish feet;
(And) I hear the sacred dogs which howl upon my track."

This whole passage then can be explained with clearness.

The young faithless swain, although he has not been cursed by the Eumolpid Priest of the Cabiri in Samothrace, nor had the long bloody (purple) robes (which those priests habitually wore) shaken out or against the threshold of his dwelling, by which he would be driven from his home and pursued to his destruction; still as the young woman whom he has abandoned—after the most solemn betrothals, and who for that reason is emphatically under the protection of those dread Divinities, the Cabiri—calls upon him with open arms, so that he appeals to his parents to know if he is not of an accursed race, he feels the full force of the curse, although the Eumolpid has not in the formal way usually pursued, cursed him and called upon the Furies to dog his steps.

THE CHARIOTEER (page 55).

This Libyan bold dear to the Emperor's soul.

The word in the original here translated *Emperor* is *Autocrator*. Under the Eastern Empire, as Bury points out in his "History of the Later Roman Empire," Autocrator got to be used as an official title of the Emperor.

The second tercet of the sestet of this sonnet is as follows in the original:
"Et tu vas voir, si l'œil d'un mortal peut suffire
A cette apothéose où fuit un char de feu,
La Victoire voler pour rejoindre Porphyre."

A stranger, who is present at the games, and who is evidently seeking information as to the names, etc., of the contestants, runs across an adherent of the Blue faction of the circus, who is willing to gratify him, and who thereupon points out to him a great charioteer of that faction in the person of the son of Calchas, who is an illustrious Libyan and a favorite of the Emperor. While he is talking the race begins, but he still makes running comments, and at its close enthusiastically joins in the acclaim to the victor. Then in the language of extravagance, carried away by the exaltation of the moment, and being perhaps something of a poet, he exclaims to the stranger that if mortal eye can suffice for the blaze of so much glory he may see the goddess Victory in her car of fire again crowning Porphyry—the son of Calchas—as she doubtless had done more than once before. The scene might very well be laid at Constantinople during the reign of Justinian, who was not only a patron of the Blues, but was a frequent attendant on the games of the circus. Indeed, as we learn from Gibbon, the factions of the circus never before had raged as they did during his reign.

FOR VIRGIL'S SHIP (page 59).

Thus Horace (excerpt from Ode III Book I):

> Sic te Diva potens Cypri,
> Sic fratres Helenæ, lucida sidera,
>   Ventorumque regat pater
> Obstrictis aliis præter Iäpyga,
>
>   Navis, quæ tibi creditum
> Debes Virgilium, finibus Atticis
>   Reddas incolumem, precor,
> Et serves animæ dimidium meæ.

This is well rendered by Lord Lytton as follows:

> So may the goddess who rules over Cyprus,
>   So may the brothers of Helen, bright stars,
> So may the Father of Winds, while he fetters
>   All, save Iapyx, the Breeze of the West,
>
> Speed thee, O Ship, as I pray thee to render
>   Virgil, a debt duly lent to thy charge,
> Whole and intact on the Attican borders,
>   Faithfully guarding the half of my soul.

Sargent renders the passage as follows:

> So may thy course the queen of Cyprus guide,
>   So Helena's twin brethren light thy sails,
> And Æolus restrain all winds beside
>   The North-west sweeping in propitious gales;

> That thou, O ship, I earnestly implore,
>   Mayst guard the precious freightage in thy care
> And through the billows to the Attic shore,
>   Virgil, my soul's own half, in safety bear.

It is interesting to compare with these the inferior version of Gladstone:

> So may the Queen of Cyprian heights,
> So Helen's brethren, starry lights,
> So speed thy course the Lord of wind,
> And all, save Zephyr, fastly bind:

> O Ship, thou hast a debt to pay
> Our Virgil: hold him well I pray,
> Unharmed to Attic bounds consign,
> And save that life, the half of mine.

TO SEXTIUS (page 62).

The barque the sands has glided o'er.
The original is: "*La barque a glissé sur les sables.*" Horace's Ode (Ode IV of Book I) which furnishes the basis for this sonnet reads thus: "Trahuntque siccas machinæ carinas"—literally, And the machines [or engines] draw the dry keels [or boats.] That is, the vessels, which, during the winter, have been hauled upon the shore for safety, are, now that spring has come, drawn into the water.

LUPERCUS (page 72).

Martial's Epigram in the original is as follows.

IN LUPERCUM

Occurris quoties, Luperce, nobis,
Vis mittam puerum, subinde dicis,
Cui tradas Epigrammaton libellum,
Lectum quem tibi protinus remittam?
Non est, quod puerum, Luperce, vexes.
Longum est, si velit ad Pyrum venire,
Et scalis habito tribus, sed altis.
Quod quæris, propius petas licebit:
Argi nempe soles subire letum.
Contra Cæsaris est forum taberna,
Scriptis postibus hinc et inde totis,
Omnes ut cito perlegas Poëtas.
Illinc me pete; ne roges Atrectum:
Hoc nomen dominus gerit tabernæ.
De primo dabit, alterove nido,
Rasum pumice, purpuraque, cultum,
Denariis tibi quinque Martialem.
Tanti non es, ais? sapis, Luperce.

The following translation may be ventured on:

TO LUPERCUS

How often, Lupercus, when meeting,
You ask, may I to thee my servant
Not send for little book where sparkle
Thy Epigrams the very latest,
Which read I shall at once return thee?—
But thus the boy you should not harass:
For long the road he'll find to Pyrum,*
And at my house three flights of stairway.
Why seek, when near is all you wish for:
Of course you know the Argiletum,*
And often there are wont to wander.
'Gainst Cæsar's forum is a bookshop,
Whose posts are covered so with titles,
One may the poets scan right quickly.
There seek me; you may ask Atrectus—
The name of him who is the master.
From his first shelf or from some other,
With pumice smoothed and clothed in purple,
For five denarii he'll give you Martial.
Too much, you say, for such a little?
O Lupercus, how wise I find you!

---

*Pyrum was the region of Rome in which Martial lived, and Argiletum was a region famous for bookshops.

THE BEAUTIFUL VIOLE (page 100).

The original, from which the poet has taken for motto the first three lines is as follows:

D'UN VANNEUR DE BLE AUX VENTS.

A vous trouppe legère
 Qui d'aile passagère
 Par le monde volez,
 Et d'un sifflant murmure
 L'ombrageuse verdure
 Doulcement esbranlez,

J'offre ces violettes,
 Ces lis *&* ces fleurettes,
 Et ces roses icy,
 Ces vermeillettes roses
 Sont freschement ecloses,
 Et ces œlliets aussi.

De vostre doulce haleine
 Eventez ceste plaine
 Eventez ce sejour ;
 Ce pendant que j'ahanne
 A mon blé que je vanne
 A la chaleur du jour.

This may be translated as follows:

FROM A WINNOWER OF GRAIN TO THE WINDS.

Nimble troop, to you
    That on light pinion through
    The world forever pass,
    And with a murmuring sweet
    Where shade and verdure meet
    Toss gently leaf and grass,

I give these violets,
    Lilies and flowerets,
    And roses here that blow;
    All these red-blushing roses
    Whose freshness now uncloses,
    And these rich pinks also.

With your soft breath now deign
    To fan the spreading plain,
    And fan, too, this retreat,
    Whilst I with toil and strain
    Winnow my golden grain
    In the day's scorching heat.

Andrew Lang's beautiful version, as taken from his "Ballads and Lyrics of Old France" (1872) is as follows:

HYMN TO THE WINDS.

The winds are invoked by the Winnowers of Corn.

DU BELLAY, 1550.

> To you, troop so fleet,
> That with winged wandering feet,
>   Through the wide world pass,
> And with soft murmuring
> Toss the green shades of spring
>   In woods and grass,
> Lily and violet
> I give, and blossoms wet,
>   Roses and dew;
> This branch of blushing roses,
> Whose fresh bud uncloses,
>   Wind-flowers too.
> Ah, winnow with sweet breath,
> Winnow the holt and heath,
>   Round this retreat;
> Where all the golden morn
> We fan the gold o' the corn,
>   In the sun's heat.

We are told that the poet accompanied his relative Cardinal du Bellay to Rome in 1552 where he remained for nearly five years. Among his poems is a series of sonnets addressed to one Mademoiselle de Viole.

VISION OF KHEM (page 124).

They follow Bari which the priests convey,
Of Ammon-Ra, who holds the sun at will;

    The Bari was a sacred boat in which the priests bore the image of a God or Gods. If on land, the boat was generally borne on the shoulders of the bearers. In the present instance the Bari, with the image of the God Ammon-Ra seated in it, is conveyed by the priests at the head of the imaginary procession.

THE SAMURAI (page 128).

This was a man with two swords.

    A fully equipped Samurai had two swords—a long one with which to do his fighting, and a short one for the hara-kiri.

BRITTANY (page 142).

Voluptuous Is and mighty Occismor.

    Professor F. V. Paget of the University of the State of California tells me that Is and Occismor were two old cities of Brittany which were destroyed by extraordinary tidal waves near the middle of the fifth century.

FLOWERY SEA (page 143).

    The inundation which seems to furnish the subject of this sonnet may have been produced by a tidal wave of some such character as that which destroyed in old time the cities of Is and Occismor.

ARMOR (page 148).

"*Sell euz ar-mor.*"
This is in the Armoric dialect and literally translated is, We have sight upon the sea; or as we might say in English, Behold the sea! Armor is from *ar*, upon; and *mor*, sea—hence Armorica.

RISING SEA (page 149).

Larousse in his Universal Dictionary of the Nineteenth Century says of the coast of Raz (mentioned in several of the sonnets): "La côte du Raz est extrêmement dangereuse, hérissée d'écueils longtemps funestes aux marins, jusqu'a l'établissement d'un phare construit il y a quelques années à côte d'un menhir. Le detroit (*raz* en breton) qui sépare le cap de l'île de Sein est d'une traversée extrêmement pénible, à cause d'un violent courant qui se porte entre le cap et l'île de Sein. De là l'adage breton dont voici la traduction littérale: *Jamais homme n'a passé le Raz sans avoir peur ou mal.*

"C'est au moment d'une tempête qu'il faut visiter le bec du Raz," dit M. Pol de Courcy. "Quoique élevé de 72 mètres au-dessus de la mer, le promontoire semble à chaque instant prêt à s'engloutir sous les vagues; une écume salée vous couvre, et des rugissements horribles dans les cavernes des rochers étourdissent à donner le vertige."

(The coast of Raz is extremely dangerous, as it bristles with reefs which for a long time were fatal to mariners until the establishment of a lighthouse constructed some years ago in the form of a menhir. The strait (raz in the Breton) which separates the cape from the isle of Sein is very difficult in the passage by reason of a violent current which runs between the cape and the isle of Sein. There is a Breton adage of which the following is a literal translation: *No man ever passed Raz without feeling fear or suffering harm.*

"It is in the moment of tempest when one should visit the beak of Raz," says M. Pol de Courcy. "Although at an elevation of some 72 metres above the sea, it seems as though at each moment the promontory might be engulfed in the waves; a salted foam covers you, and the horrible roarings in the caverns of the rocks are so deafening as to make one dizzy.")

INDEX

After Cannæ	74
After Petrarch	98
Ancestor, The	117
Andromeda with the Monster	37
Antique Medal	135
Antony and Cleopatra	81
Ariadne	28
Armor	148
Artemis	21
Awakening of a God, The	30
Bacchanal	29
Bath, The	146
Bath of the Nymphs, The	25
Beautiful Viole, The	100
Bed, The	152
Beech-Tree God, The	87
Birth of Aphrodite, The	15
Brittany	142
Celestial Blazon	147
Centauress, The	12
Centaurs and Lapithæ	13
Century Flower	131
Charioteer, The	55
Chase, The	22
Church Window	93

Claudius Popelin, To	107
Conquerors, The	113
Coral Reef	132
Cydnus, The	79
Daimio, The	129
Dead City, To a	120
Death of the Eagle	153
Divine Mountains, To the	88
Dogaressa, The	103
Dreams of Enamel	109
Enamel	108
Epiphany	94
Epitaph	101
Evening of Battle	80
Exiled, The	89
Flight of the Centaurs	14
Flowers of Fire	130
Flowery Sea	143
Flute, The	61
For Virgil's Ship	59
Founder of a City, To a	118
Funeral	136
Funerary Epigram	46
Gilded Vellum	102
Goatherd, The	43
God of the Gardens, The	63
I	65
II	66
III	67
IV	68
V	69

Hermes Criophorus, To	51
Husbandman, The	50
In the Time of Charles Fifth, Emperor	116
Inscription	111
Jason and Medea	16
José-Maria de Heredia, To	1
Life of the Dead	155
Little Villa, A	60
Lupercus	72
Magician, The	31
Marsyas	33
Medal	96
Michelangelo	157
More Beyond	154
Nemea	9
Nessus	11
NOTES:	
Armor	172
Brittany	171
Flowery Sea	171
For Virgil's Ship	164
Lupercus	166
Rising Sea	172
To Sextius	165
The Beautiful Viole	168
The Charioteer	163
The Magician	161
Nymphæa	23

Oblivion	5
Old Goldsmith, The	105
On a Broken Marble	158
On Othrys	56
On the Book of Loves of Pierre de Ronsard	99
On the Old-Bridge	104
Painter, A	141
Pan	24
Perseus and Andromeda	38
Pindar, Extract from	XV
Prayer of Death, The	48
Preface	V
Prisoner, The	127
Rapier, The	97
Ravishment of Andromeda, The	39
Regilla	53
Rising Sea	149
Rossi, To the Tragedian	156
Runner, The	54
Same, To the	119
Samurai, The	128
Sea Breeze	150
Sextius, To	62
Shell, The	151
Shepherds, The	44
Shipwreck, The	47
Slave, The	49
Siesta	138
Sphinx, The	32
Spring, The	86
Star of the Sea	145

Stymphalus	10
Sunset	144
Sword, The	106
Table of Contents	IX
Tepidarium	70
Thermodon, The	17
Tomb of the Conqueror	115
Tranquillus	71
Trebia, The	73
Triumpher, To a	75
Vase, The	27
Vintage	137
Vision of Khem, *I*	123
II	124
III	125
Votive Epigram	45
Vow, The	85
Wood-worker of Nazareth, The	95
Youth	114
Youthful Dead, The	52

www.ingramcontent.com/pod-product-compliance
Lightning Source LLC
Chambersburg PA
CBHW020238170426
43202CB00008B/133